CONTENTS

Words in **bold** are explained in the glossary.

What is an orang-utan?

Orang-utans are big **apes**.

They live in the **rainforests** of South-east Asia.

They live high up in the trees.

Orang-utan

World map

Gibbons, gorillas and chimpanzees
are also apes.

Gorilla

Gibbon

Chimpanzee

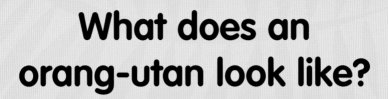

What does an orang-utan look like?

Orang-utans have shaggy, red hair and long arms.

They don't have tails.

A young orang-utan has light rings around its eyes.

A mother orang-utan

A father orang-utan is much bigger than a mother orang-utan.

He has big pads on his cheeks.

A father orang-utan

Meet a baby orang-utan

This is a baby orang-utan.

He is about two years old.

He lives with his mother high up in the trees.

The baby's father lives in another part of the rainforest.

What does the baby orang-utan eat?

At first the baby orang-utan has only his mother's milk.

Later he begins to eat fruit.

His mother chews the fruit.

Then she gives it to him.

Orang-utan food

When the baby is bigger he gets his own food.

He eats **figs** and other fruit.

He eats bark, leaves, ants, snails and eggs, too.

Fruit

Ants

Snails

Orang-utans eat over 400 different kinds of food.

How does the baby get about?

The mother orang-utan has long hair.

The baby orang-utan holds on to her long hair.

He holds on as she swings
from tree to tree.

15

When does the baby go off on his own?

When the baby is bigger he begins to get about on his own.

He holds on to a branch and swings to another one.

Then he swings from tree to tree.

Making a nest

The baby orang-utan sleeps with his mother at night.

She bends branches to make a **nest** high up in the trees.

She puts leaves in the nest to make it cosy.

Orang-utans in danger

Orang-utans live in the trees in the rainforest.

The trees are cut down for their wood.

When the rainforests get smaller there are not so many trees where the orang-utans can live.

If all the trees are cut down
where will the orang-utans live?

Glossary

ape
A large primate with no tail.

figs
A type of sweet fruit, shaped like a pear and full of seeds.

nest
A treetop bed made from branches and leaves.

orang-utan
The name means 'person of the forest'.

rainforest
A tropical, thick forest that has lots of rain.

Index

Copyright © ticktock Entertainment Ltd 2008
First published in Great Britain in 2008 by ticktock Media Ltd.,
Unit 2, Orchard Business Centre, North Farm Road, Tunbridge Wells, Kent TN2 3XF
ISBN 978 1 84696 761 0 pbk
Printed in China

We would like to thank: Penny Worms, Shirley Bickler and Suzanne Baker and the National Literacy Trust.

Picture credits (t=top, b=bottom, c=centre, l-left, r=right, OFC= outside front cover)
All images courtesy of Digital Vision

Every effort has been made to trace the copyright holders, and we apologise in advance for any unintentional omissions. We would be pleased to insert the appropriate acknowledgements in any subsequent edition of this publication.